Get to know the creatures in this book!

Dunkleosteus: An armor plated 35 foot long fish from the Paleozoic era. Instead of teeth, Dunkleosteus had two bony blades, which were a part of its jaw that acted like a bear trap to catch fish.

Dimetrodon: What looks like a giant lizard with a giant sail on his back, Dimetrodon was more closely related to mammals and lived at the end of the Permian period, 250 million years ago.

Eoraptor: One of the earliest dinosaurs, this light and agile theropod was the size of a fox. Eoraptor had both sharp and broad teeth, which may indicate that Eoraptor ate both plants and animals.

Dilophosaurus: Its name means "Two crested lizard". The double crest on its head is the distinguishing feature of this Jurassic theropod.

Compsognathus: One of the smallest theropods, about the size of a chicken, this dinosaur lived during the late Jurassic period.

Allosaurus: A common large hunter of the Jurassic period with large claws and serrated teeth, this dinosaur was a top predator of its time.

Stegosaurus: This dinosaur is famous for its large bony plates along its back and its sharp spikes on the end of its tail.

Parasaurolophus: A plant eater from the late Cretaceous period, this dinosaur had a crest containing many tubes that likely worked like a trumpet to make loud calls.

Pteranodon: This animal is not a dinosaur, but a flying reptile called a pterosaur. These creatures sailed over the oceans looking for fish to eat.

Quetzalcoatlus: With a wingspan of over 30 feet, this is one of the biggest pterosaurs to have ever lived.

Tyrannosaurus Rex: Probably the most famous dinosaur of all, the T-rex is a huge predator with powerful jaws, able to crush bone. Its closest relative living today is the chicken.

Triceratops: Another very famous dinosaur, this three horned ceratopsian had a giant frill and resembled today's rhinoceros.

Velociraptor: Small and very agile, this birdlike dinosaur had the ever popular toe claw. It is now known that these creatures were covered with feathers and it is thought that they hunted in packs.

Pachysephalosaurus: It is unknown why they had such a large bony dome atop their head. It is a common belief that these dinosaurs would fight by head butting each other.

Ankylosaurus: As large as a tank and slow moving, these creatures roamed North America covered in armor and wielded a large club tail.

Archelon: An ancient giant sea turtle of the late Cretaceous period, they are the largest sea turtle on record.

Mosasuarus: An ocean reptile with very sharp pointed teeth, perfect for grasping wriggling prey.

Muttaburasaurus: A famous dinosaur named after a town in Australia, this dinosaur had a crest that could possibly be inflated like that of the hooded seal of today.

Edmontosaurus: A large hadrosaur of the late Cretaceous period, this dinosaur had very efficient chewing teeth for eating plants, but was also a favorite meal of the Tyrannosaurs.

Pachyrhinosaurus: A ceratopsian dinosaur with several horns decorating its frill and head. Fossils have been found in northern Canada, and they may have migrated south to find food in the winter.

Spinosaurus: One of the more mysterious dinosaurs to be found, they are thought to be heavier and longer than a T-rex. They preyed on fish and had a giant sail on their back.

Styracosaurus: A relative of the Triceratops, this ceratopsian dinosaur had an elongated frill decorated with long horns, making it very distinct looking.

Lambeosaurus: A large hadrosaur of the late Cretaceous period, this dinosaur is known for its "hatchet" head crest.

Corythosaurus: A hadrosaur with a crest on top of its head, which may have been used to resonate sounds for communication with other dinosaurs.

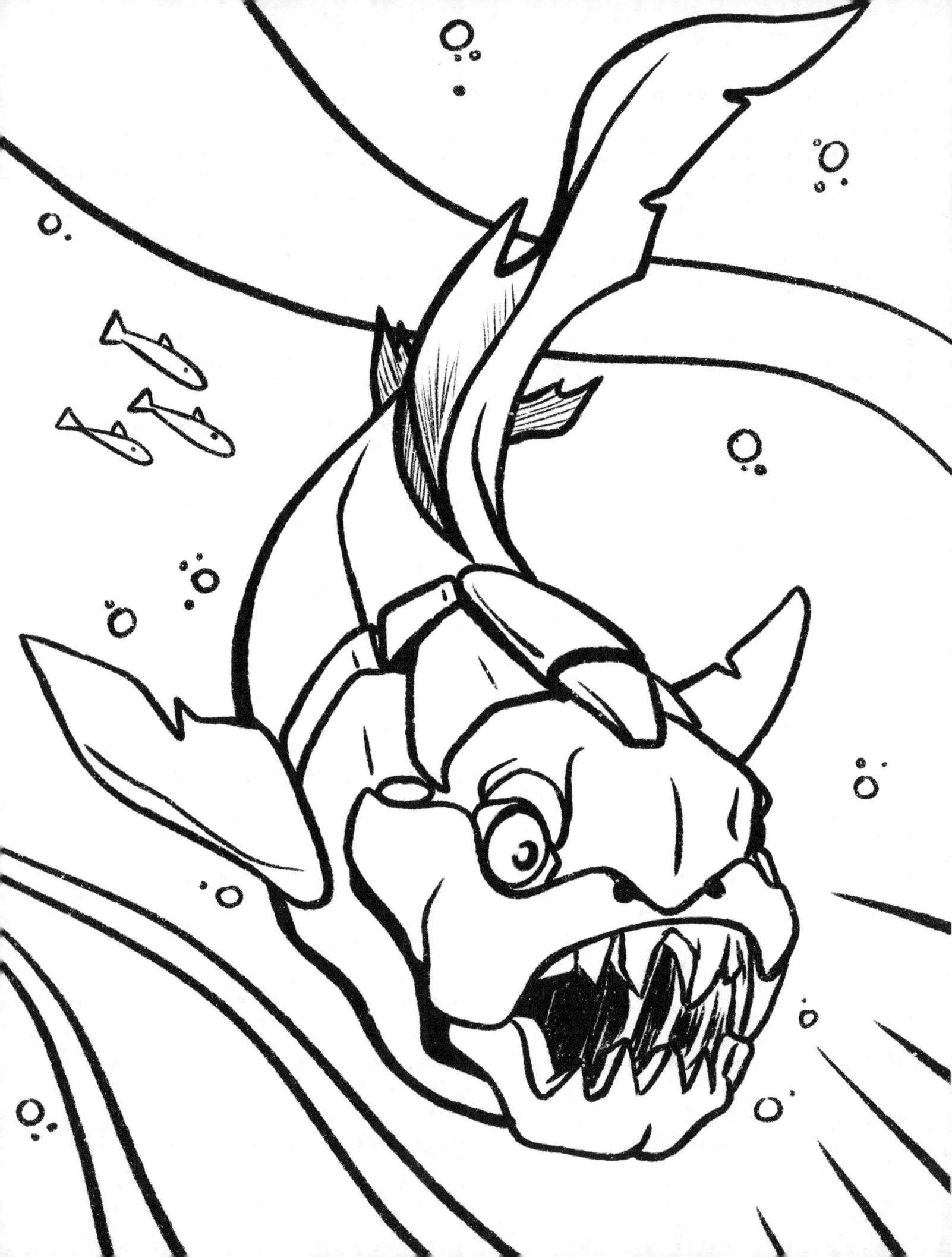

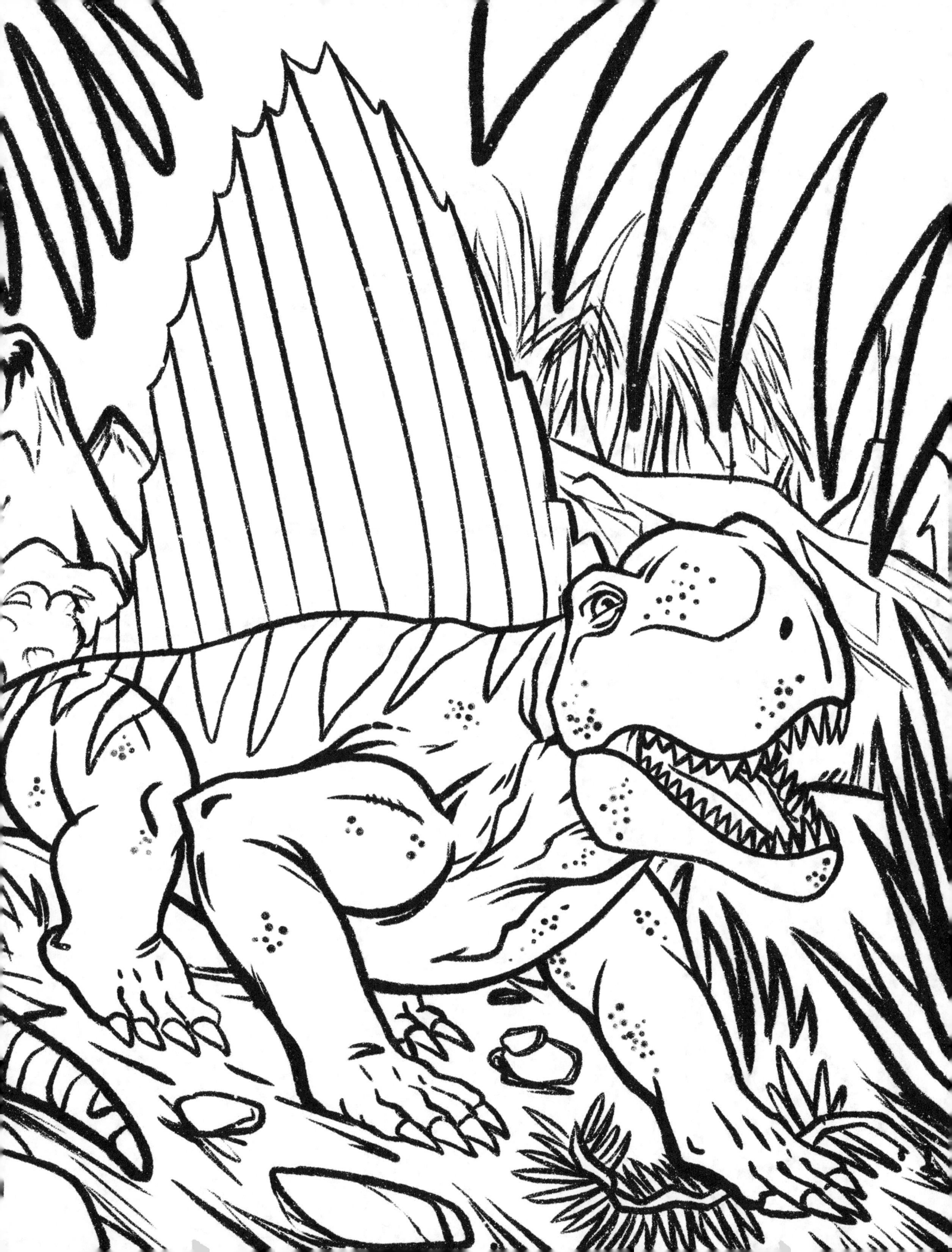

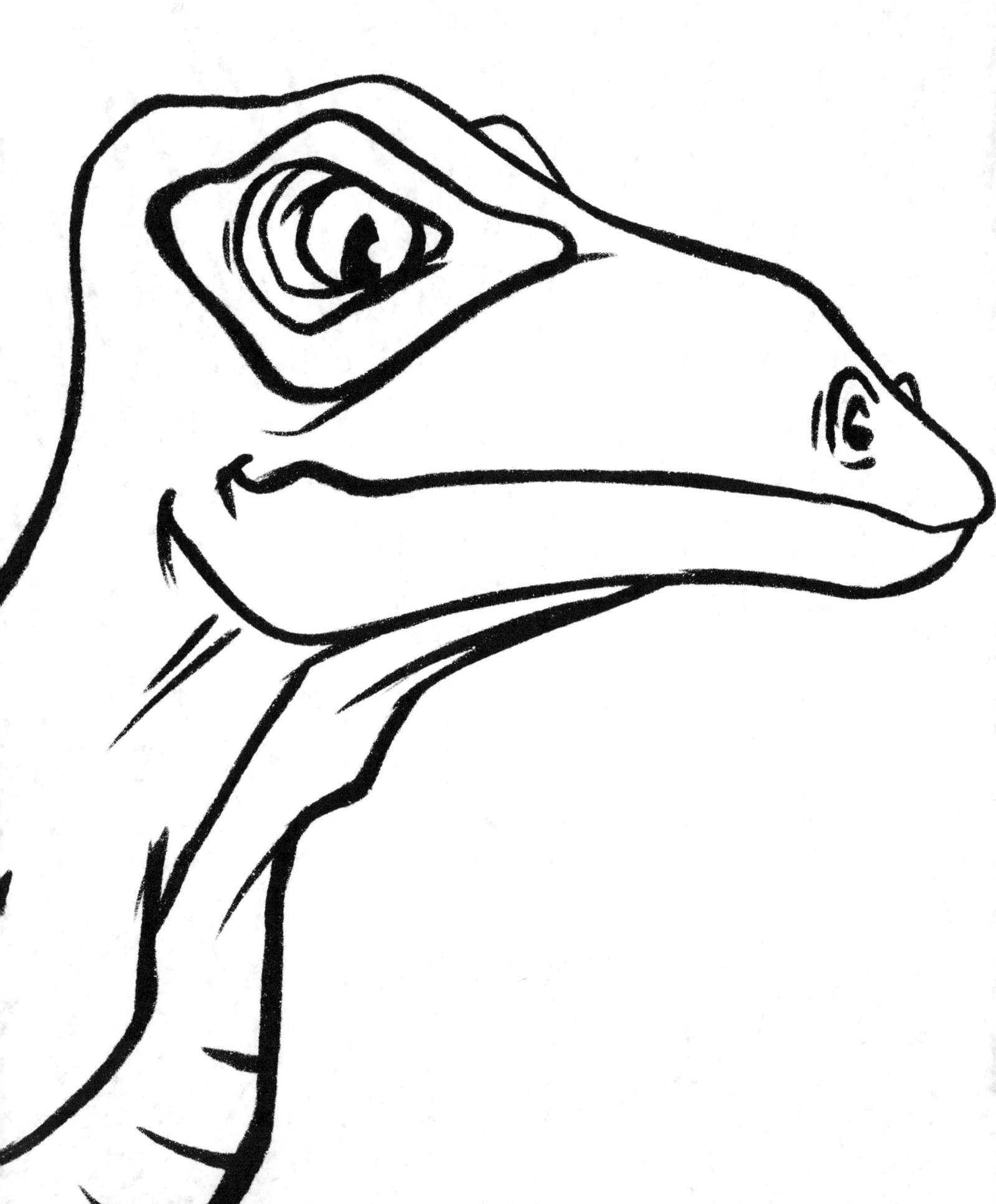

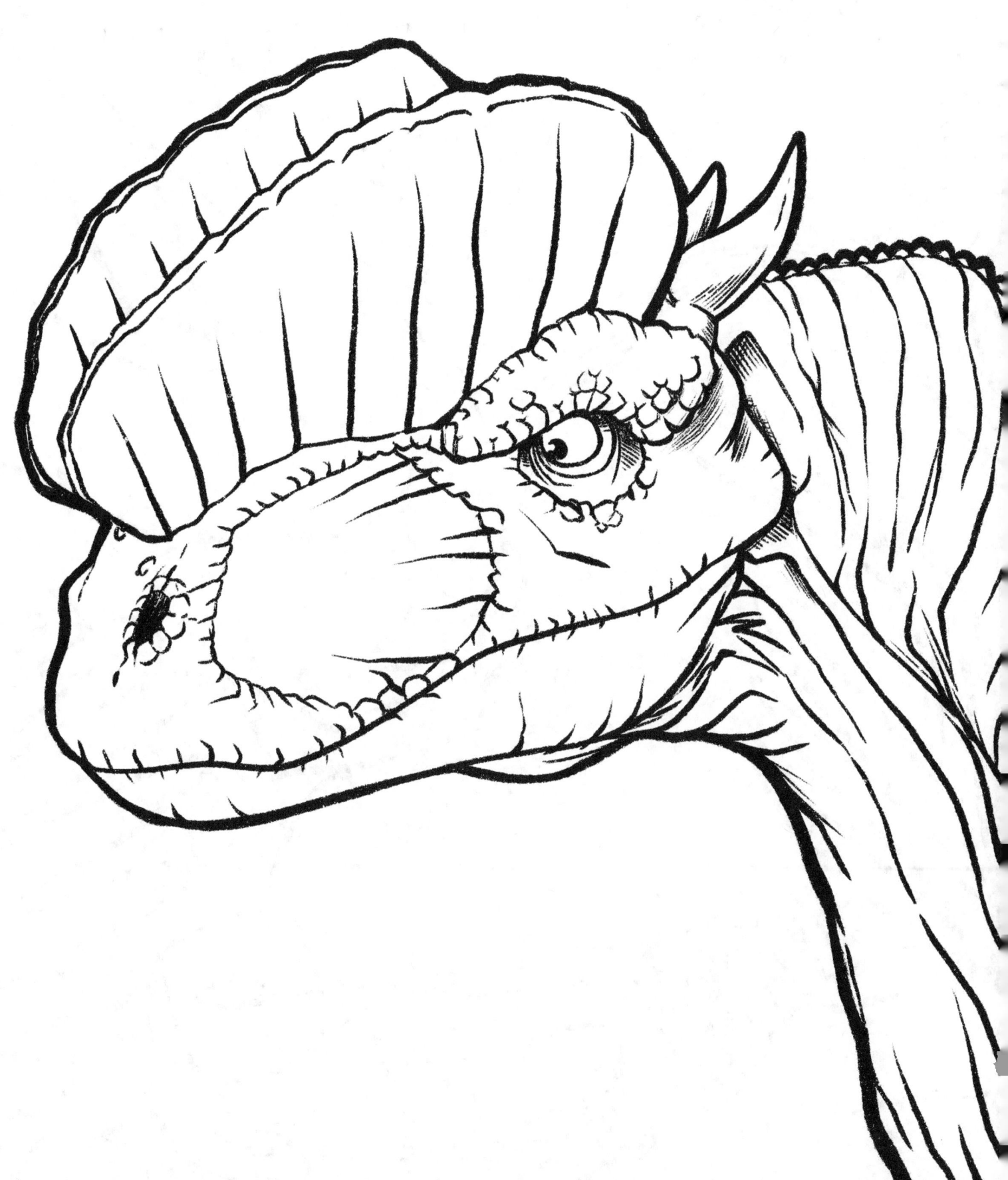

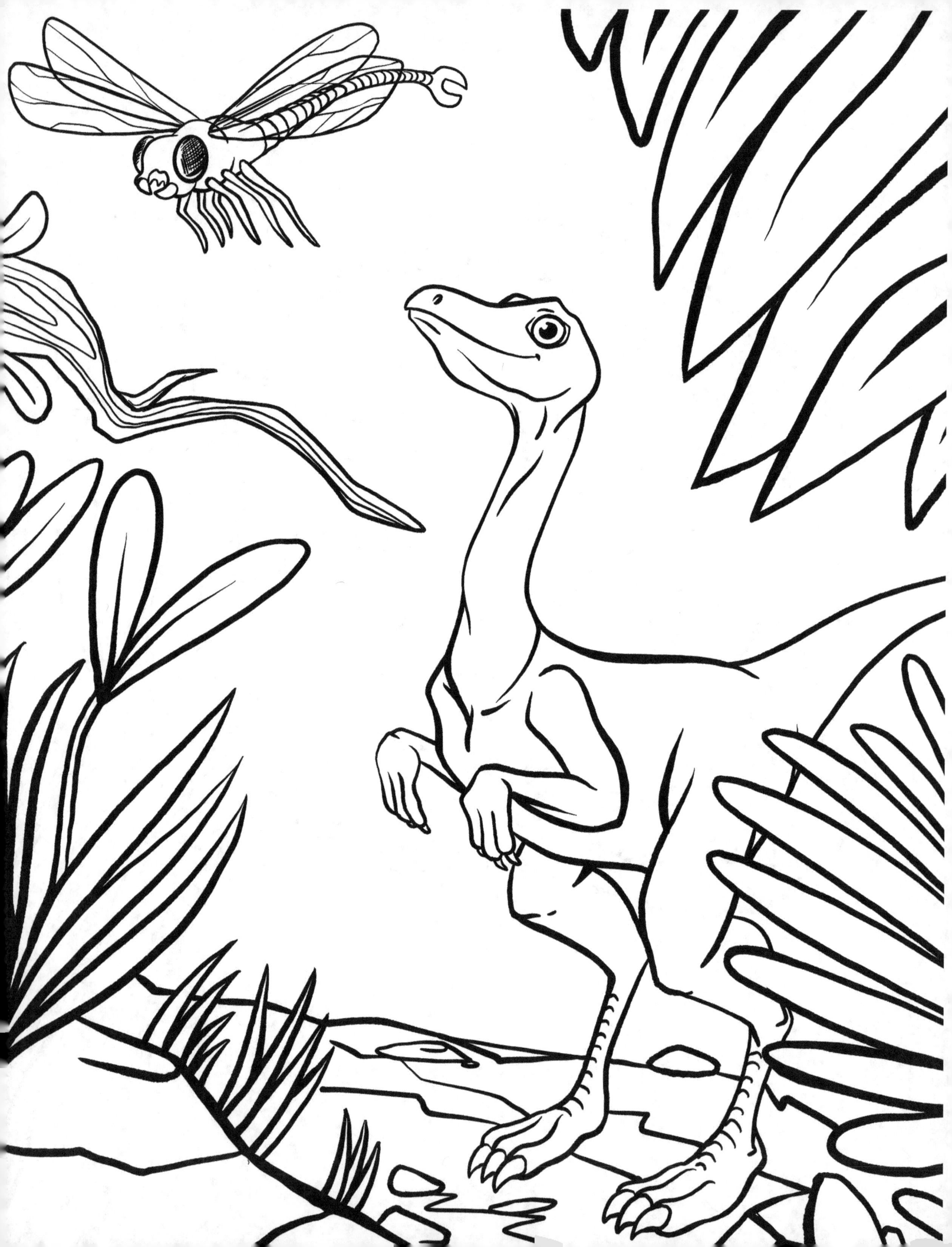

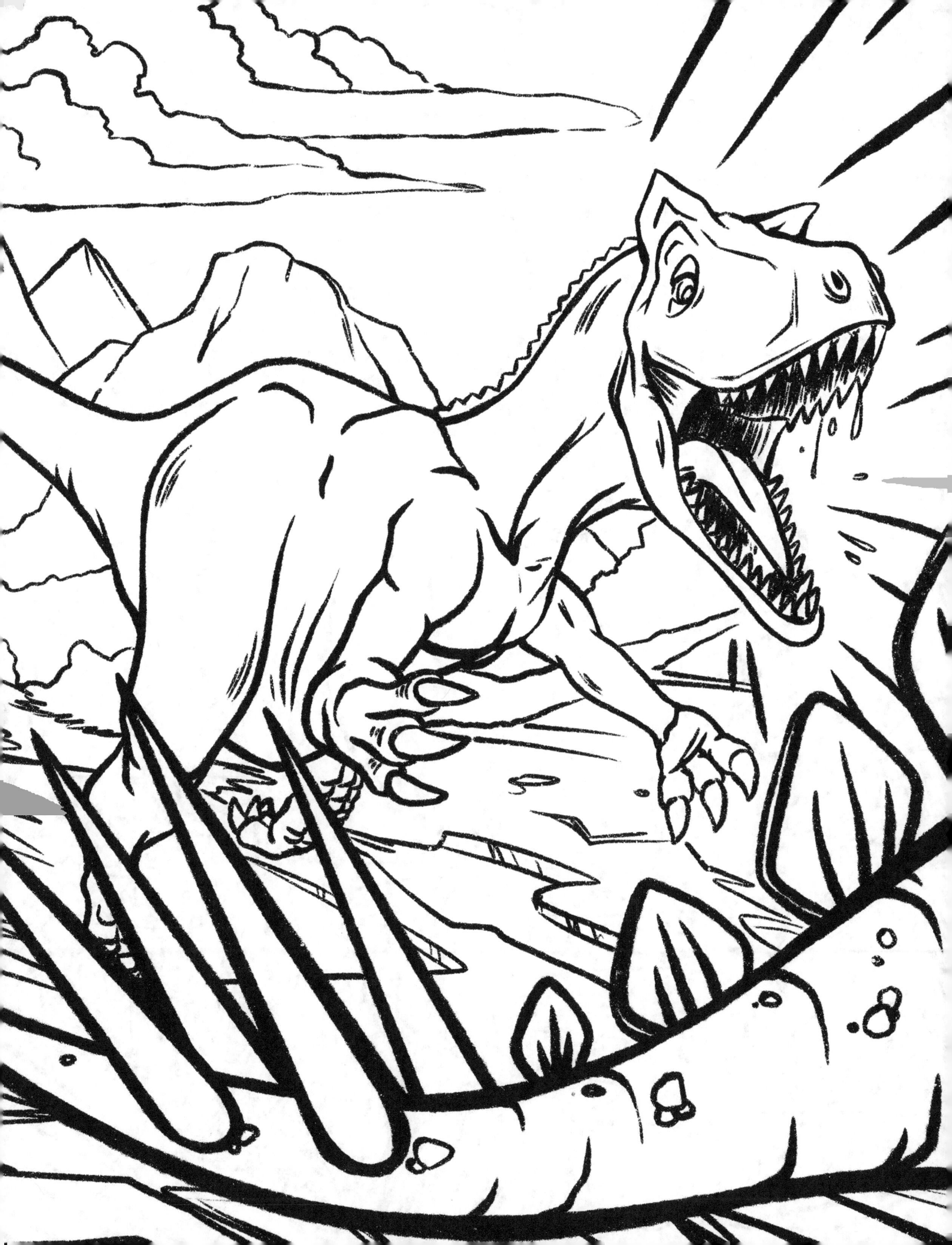

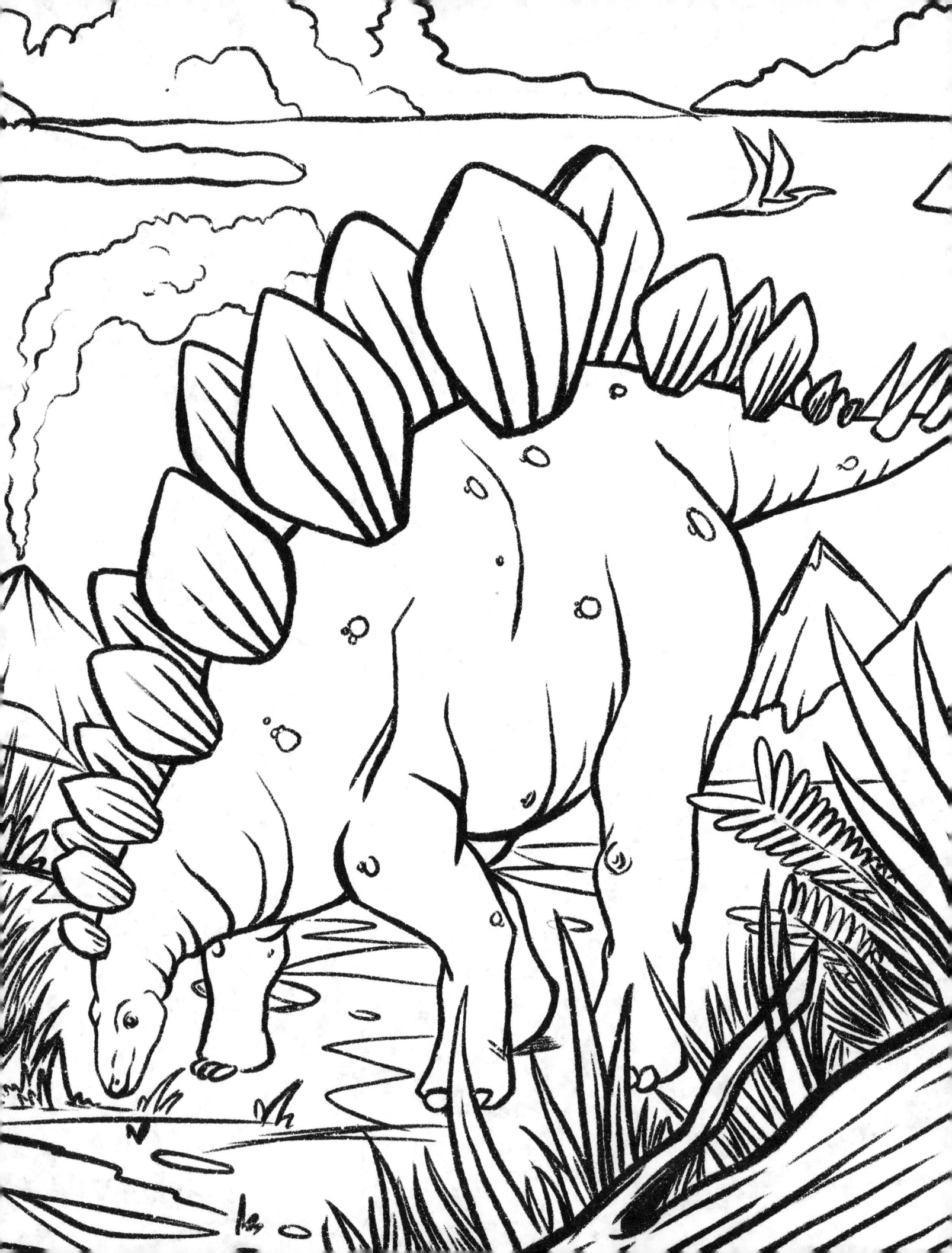

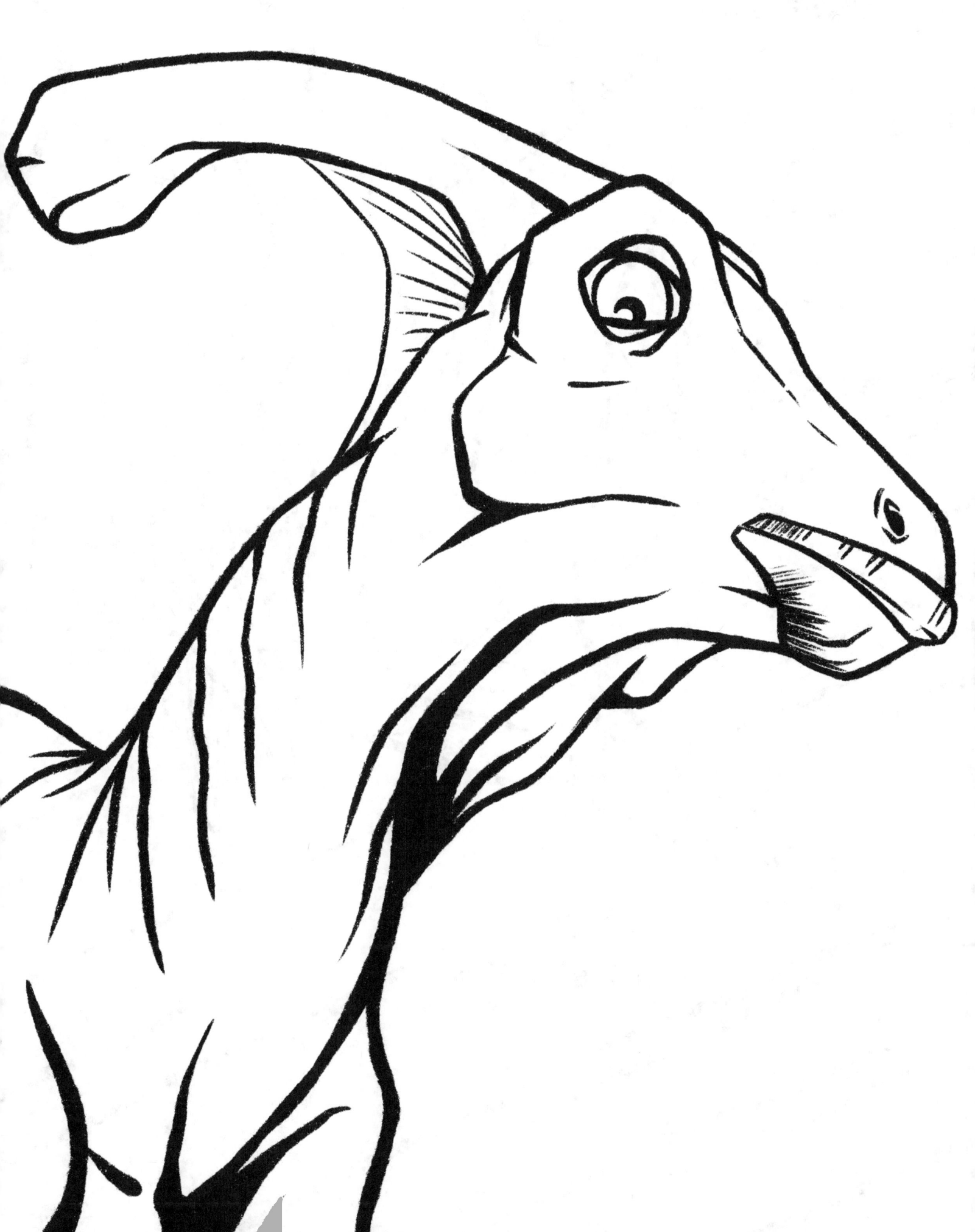

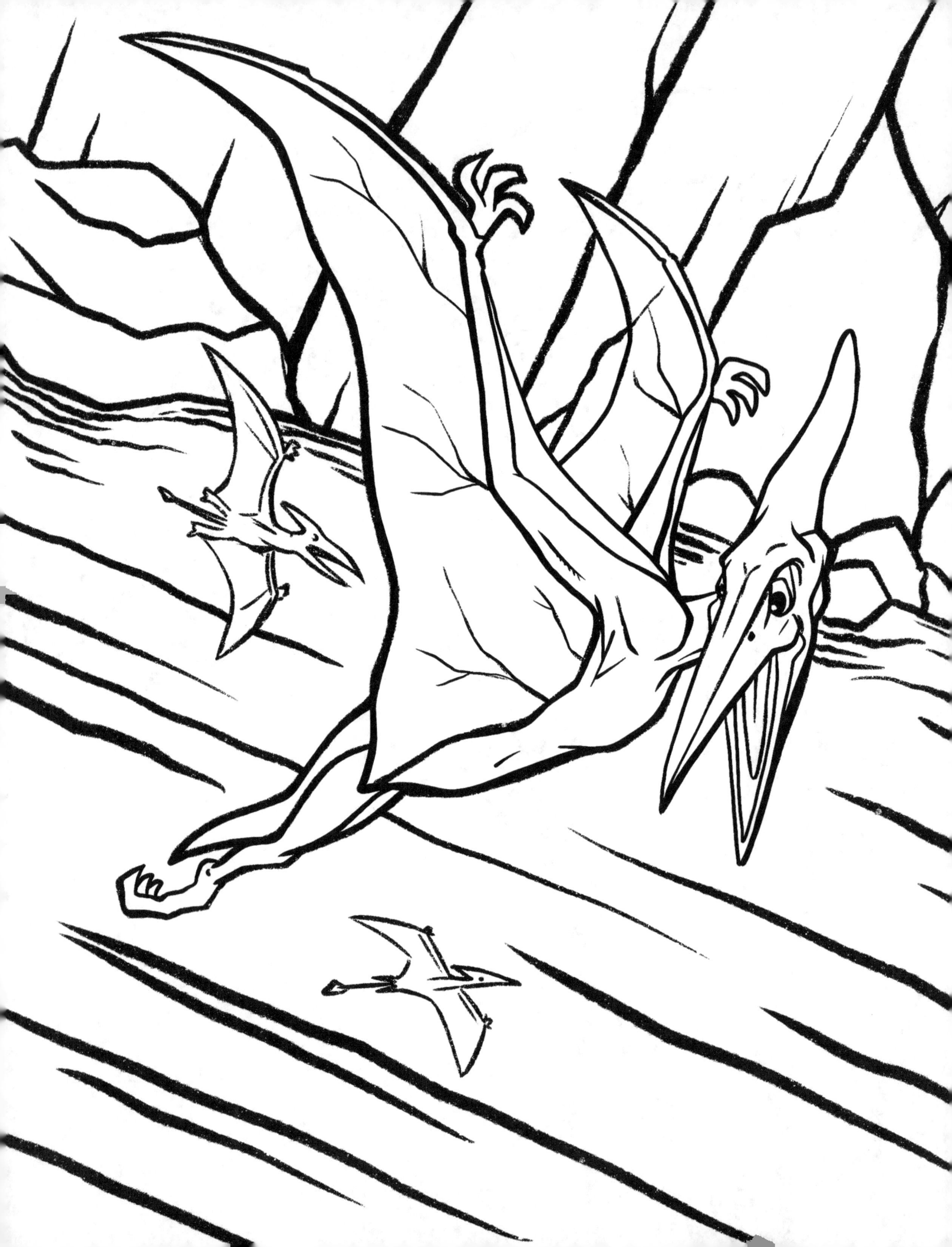

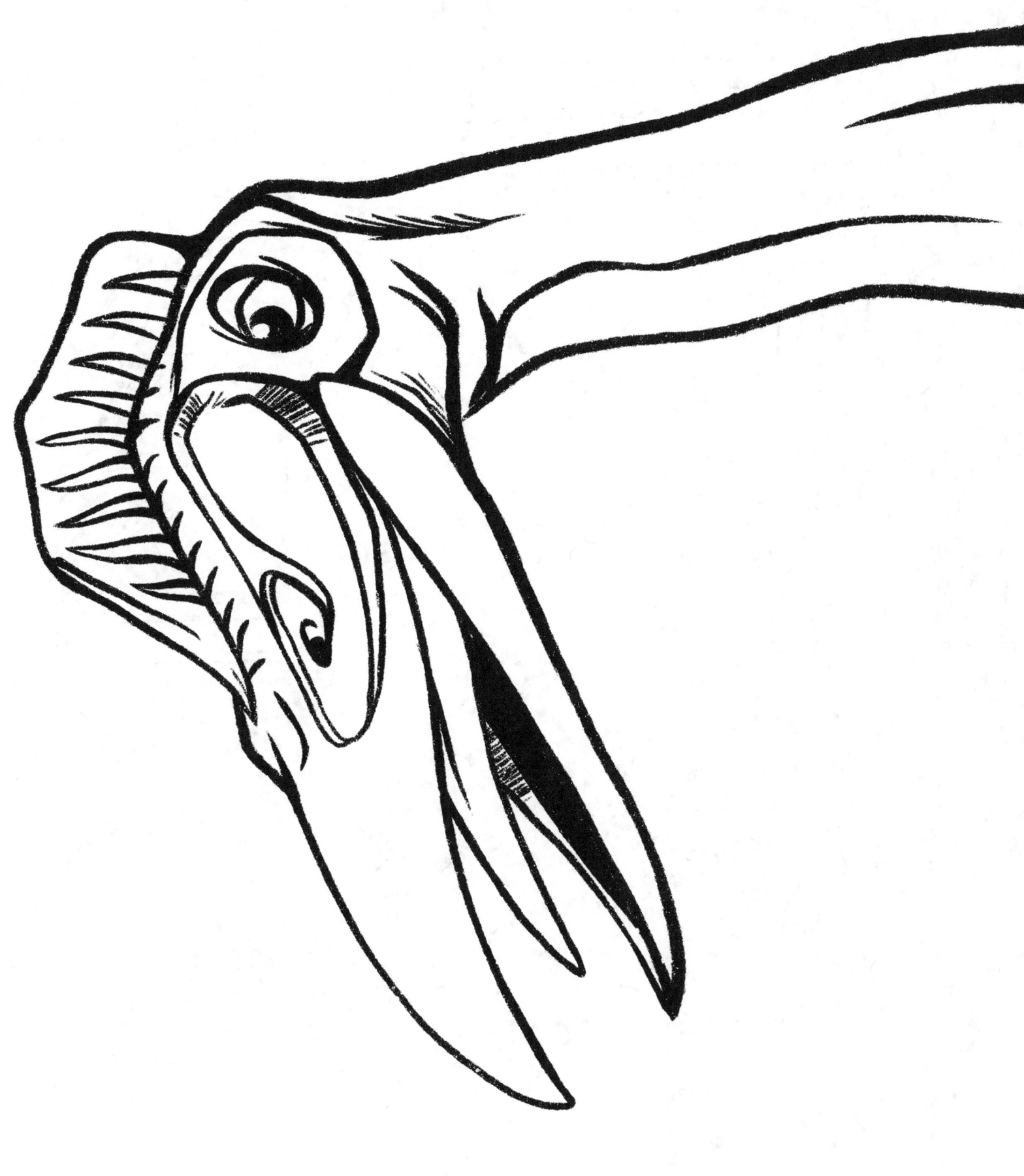

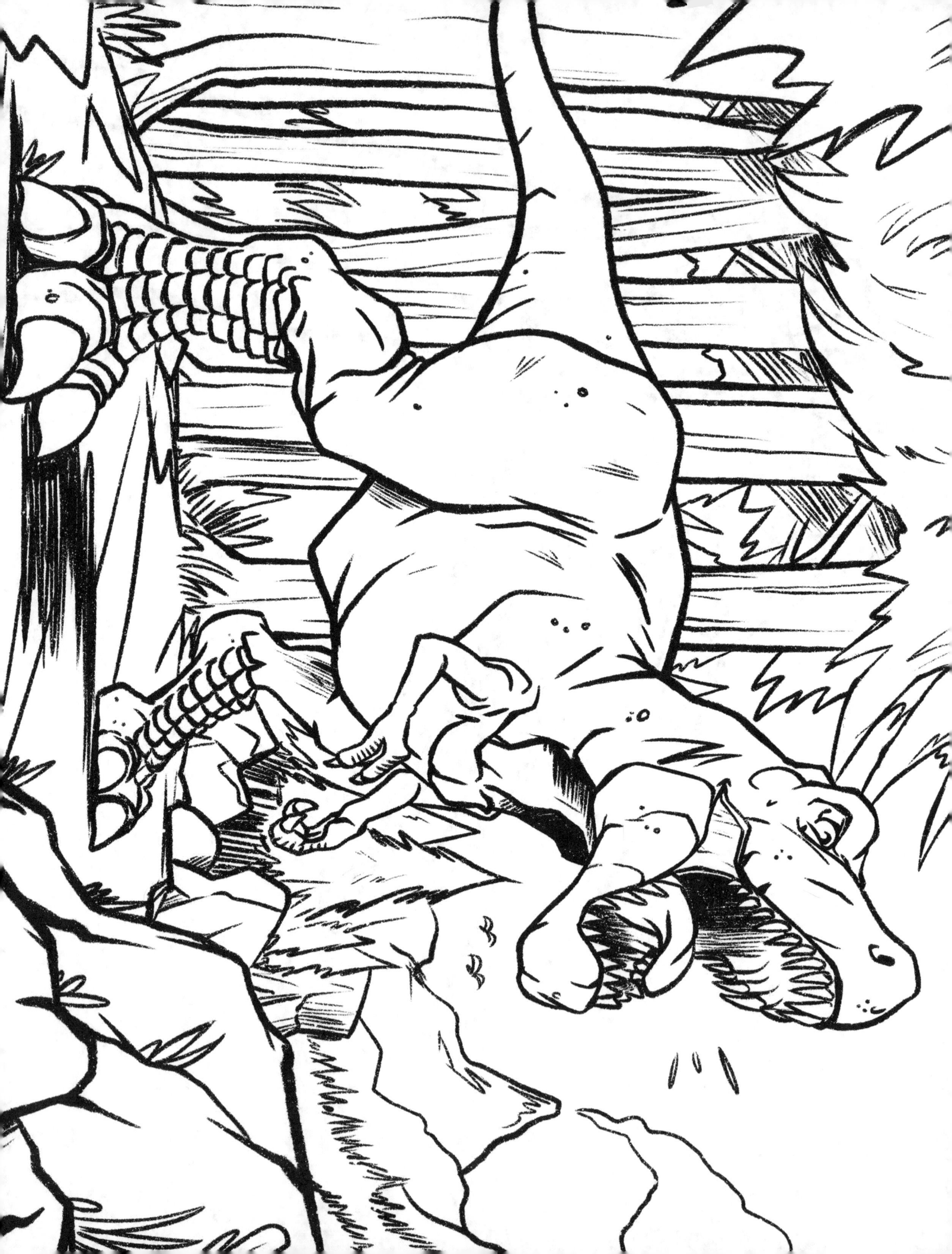

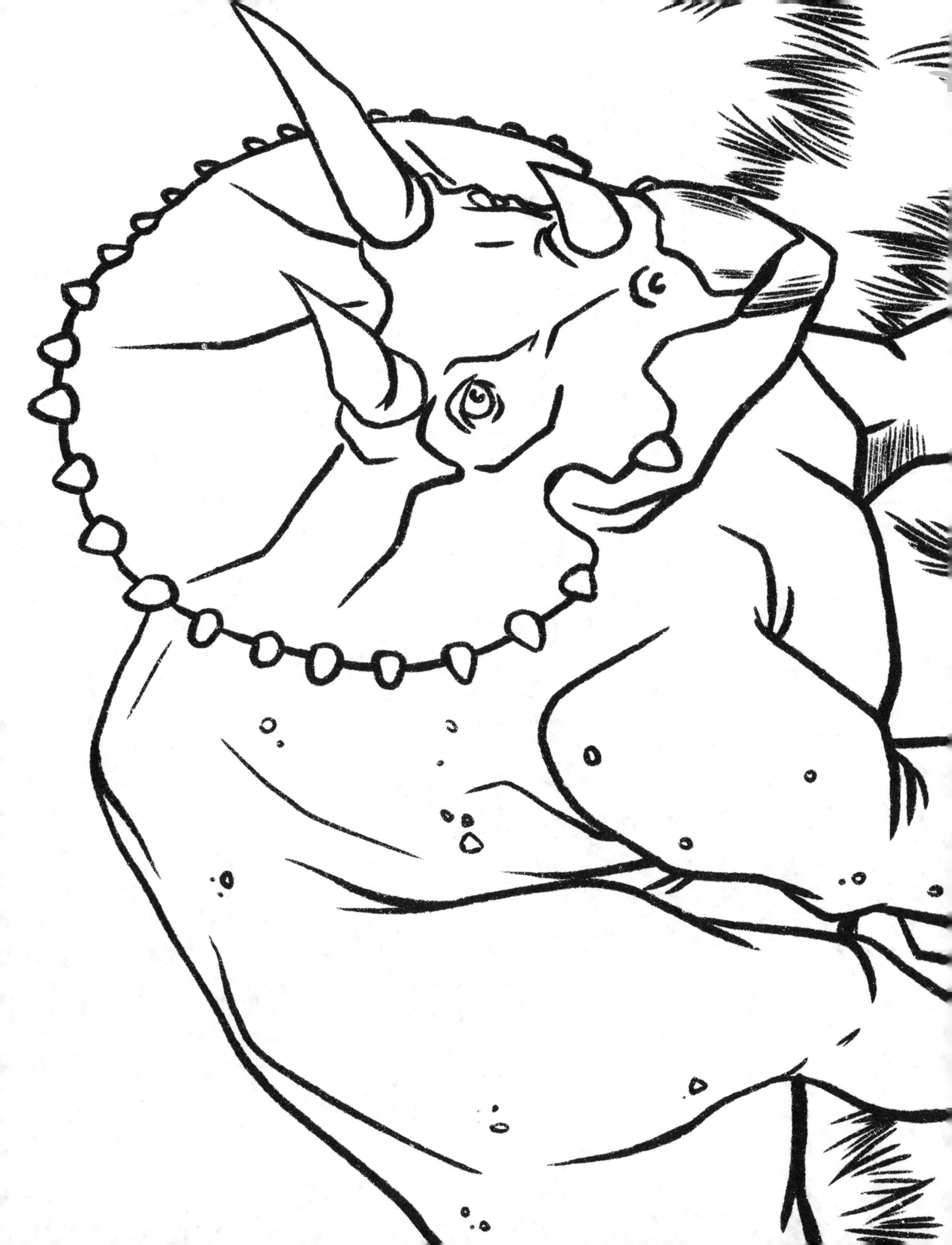

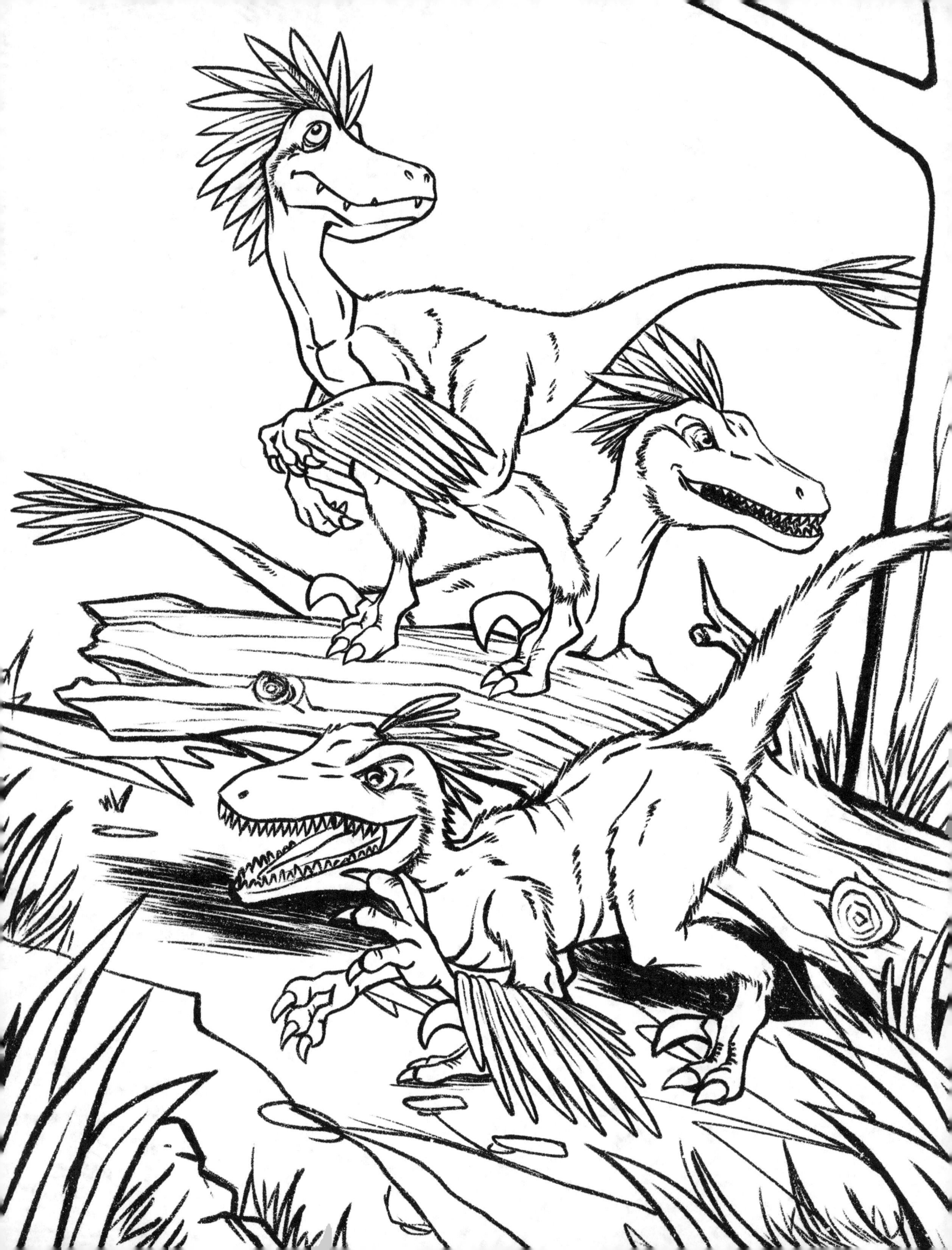

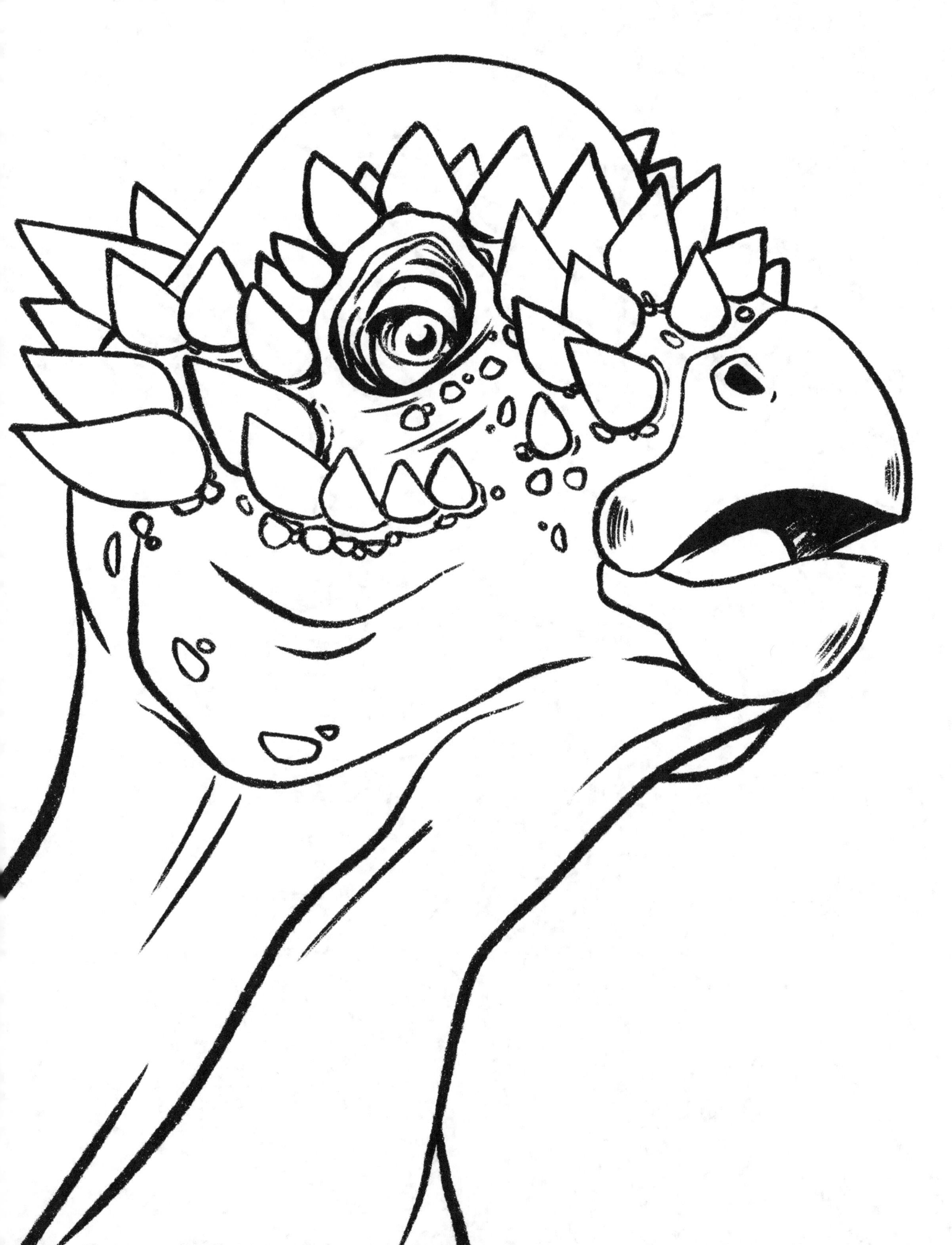

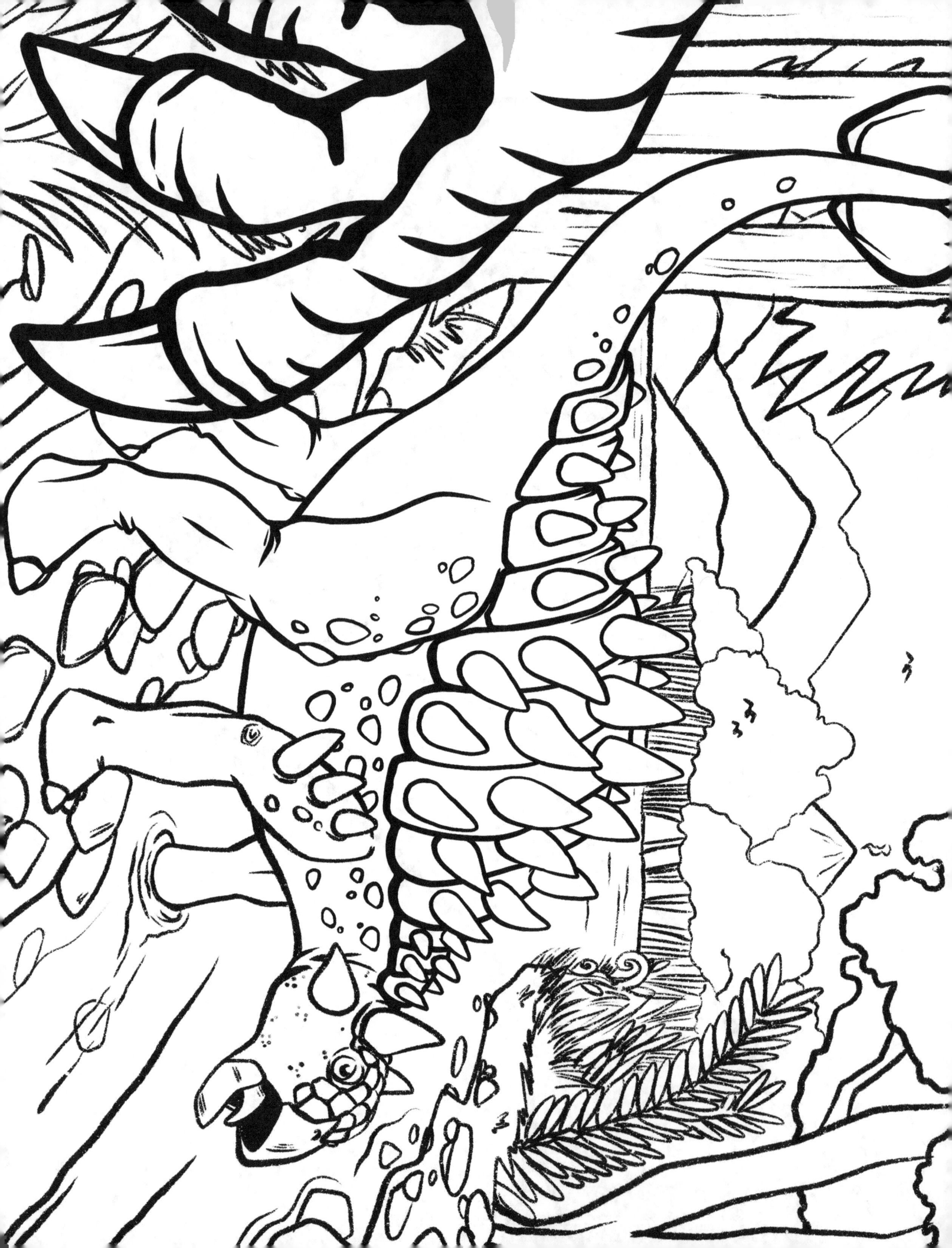

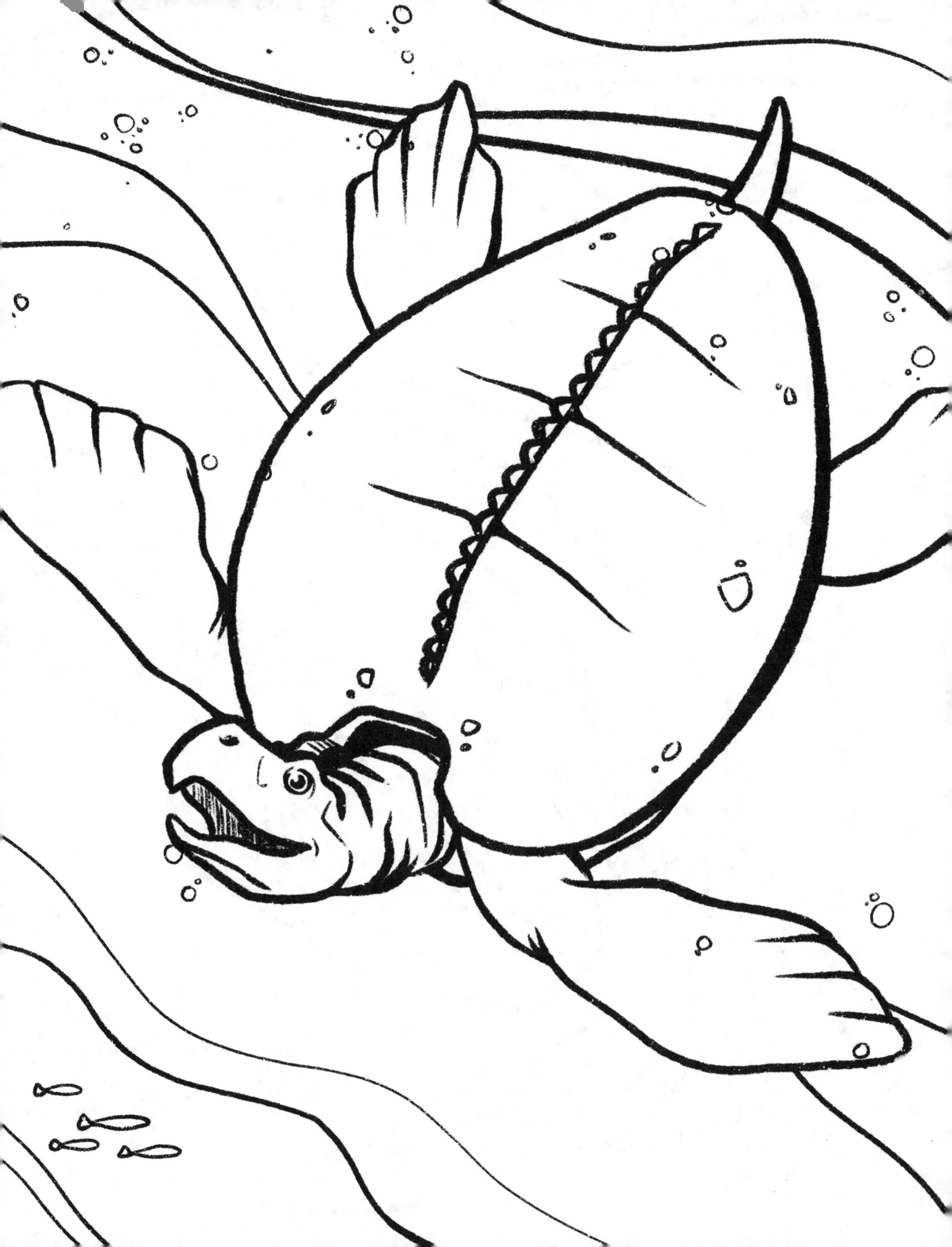

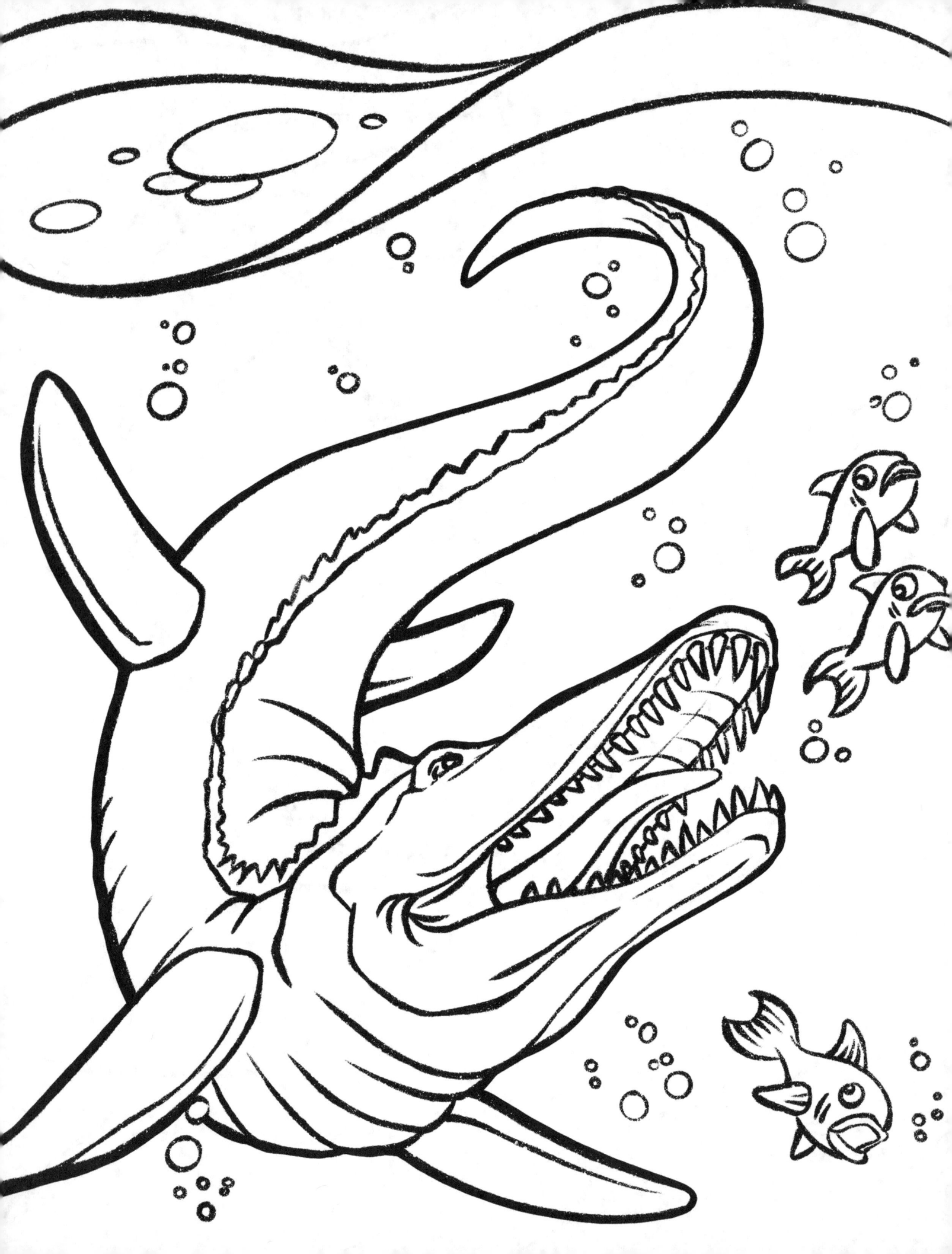

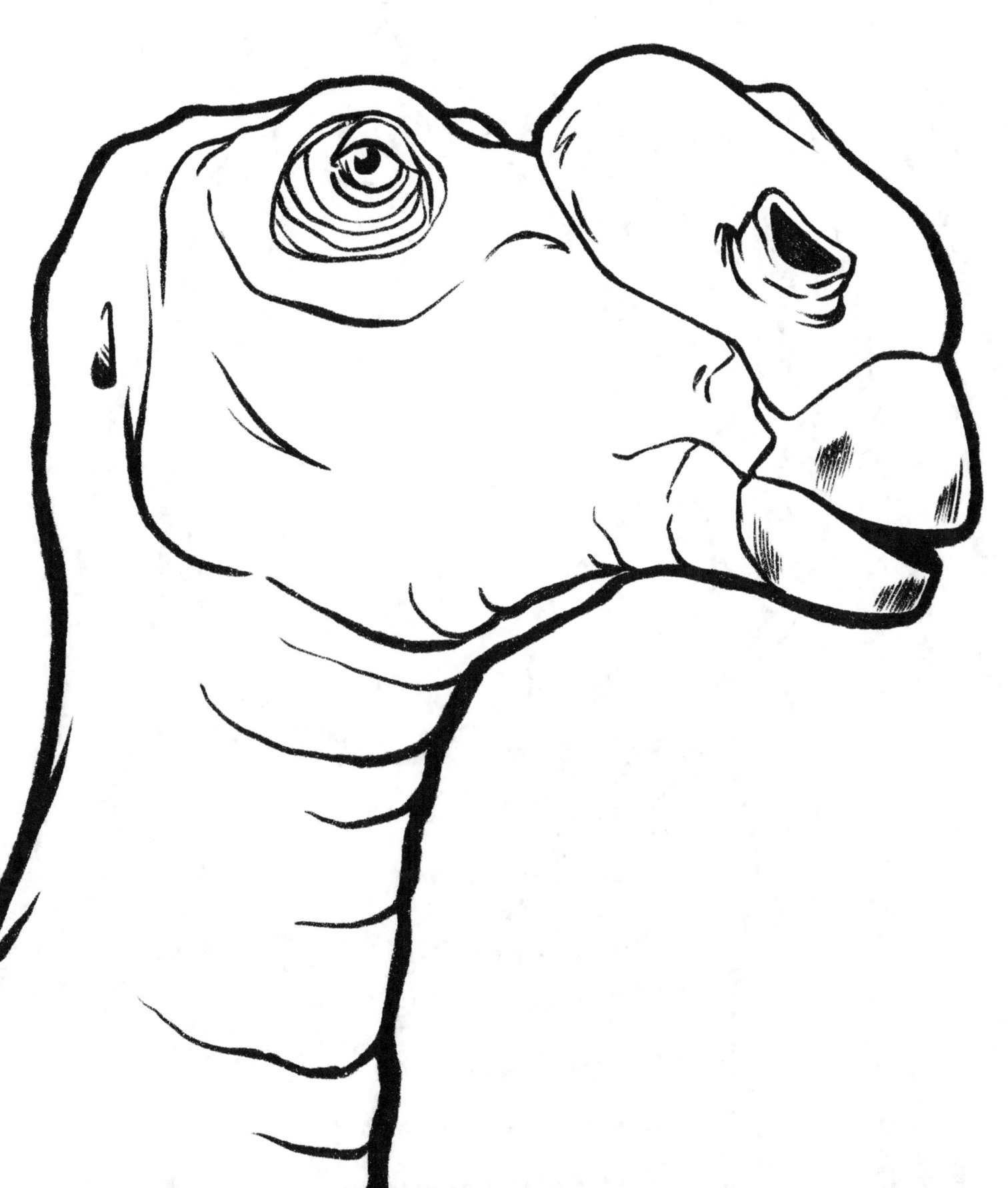

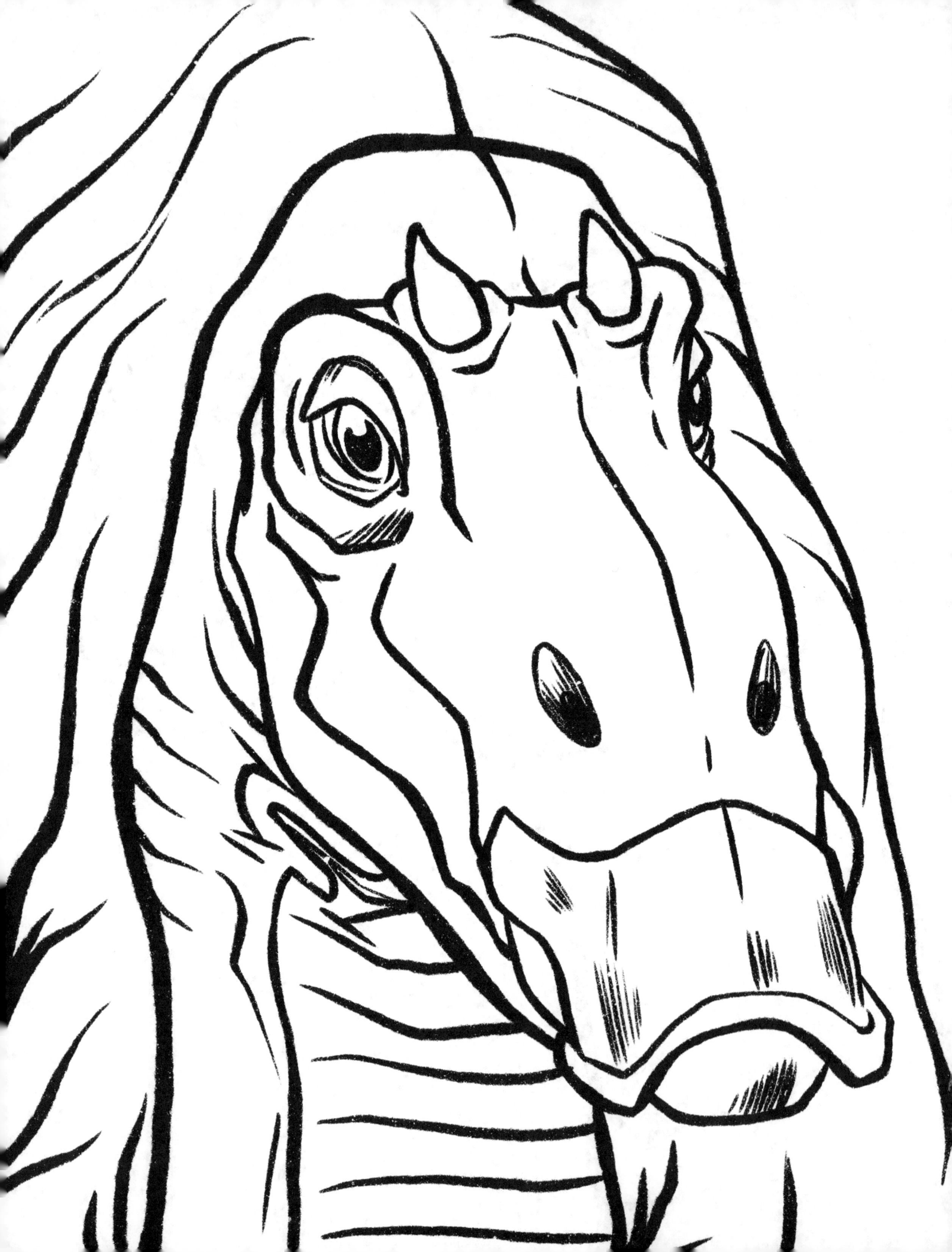

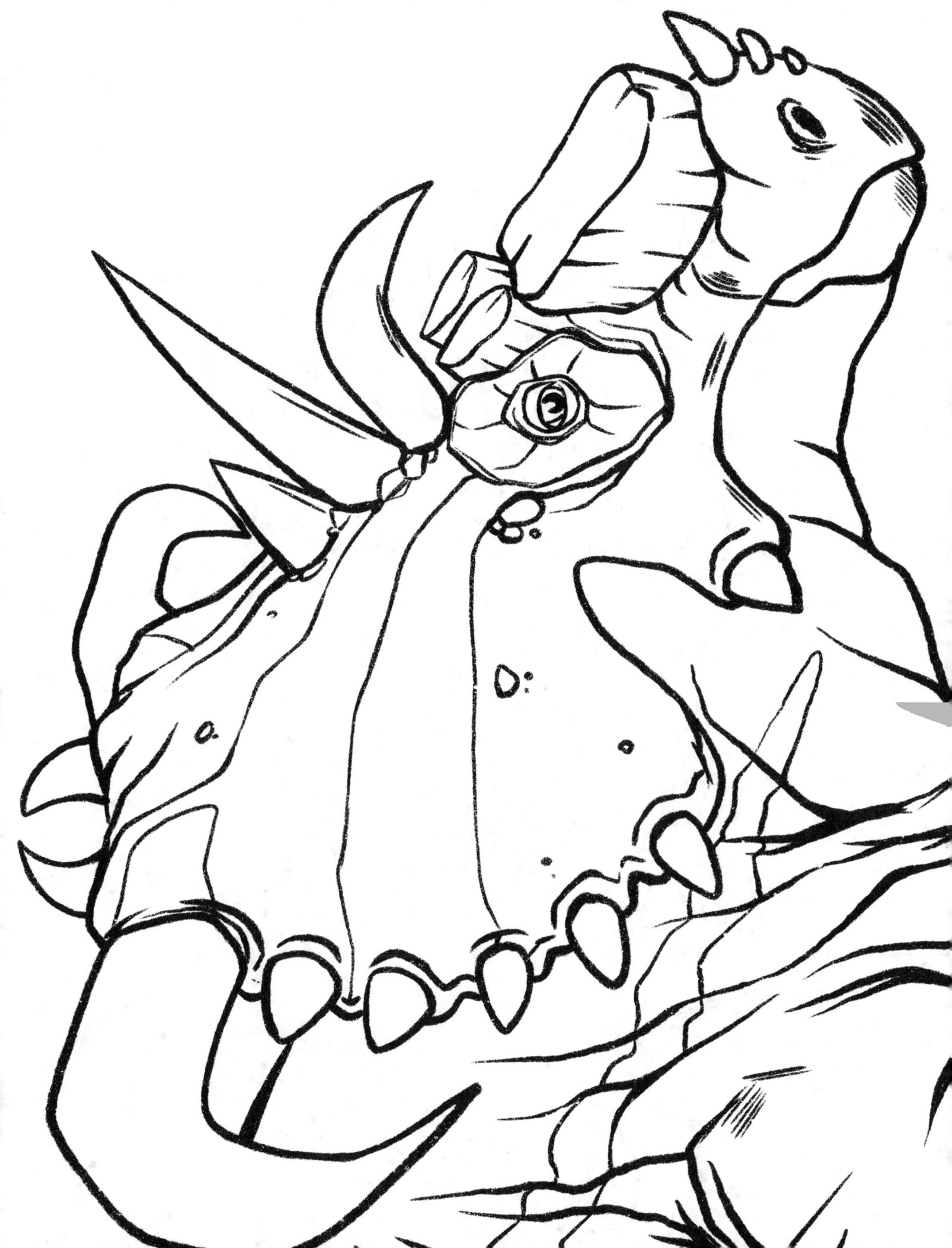

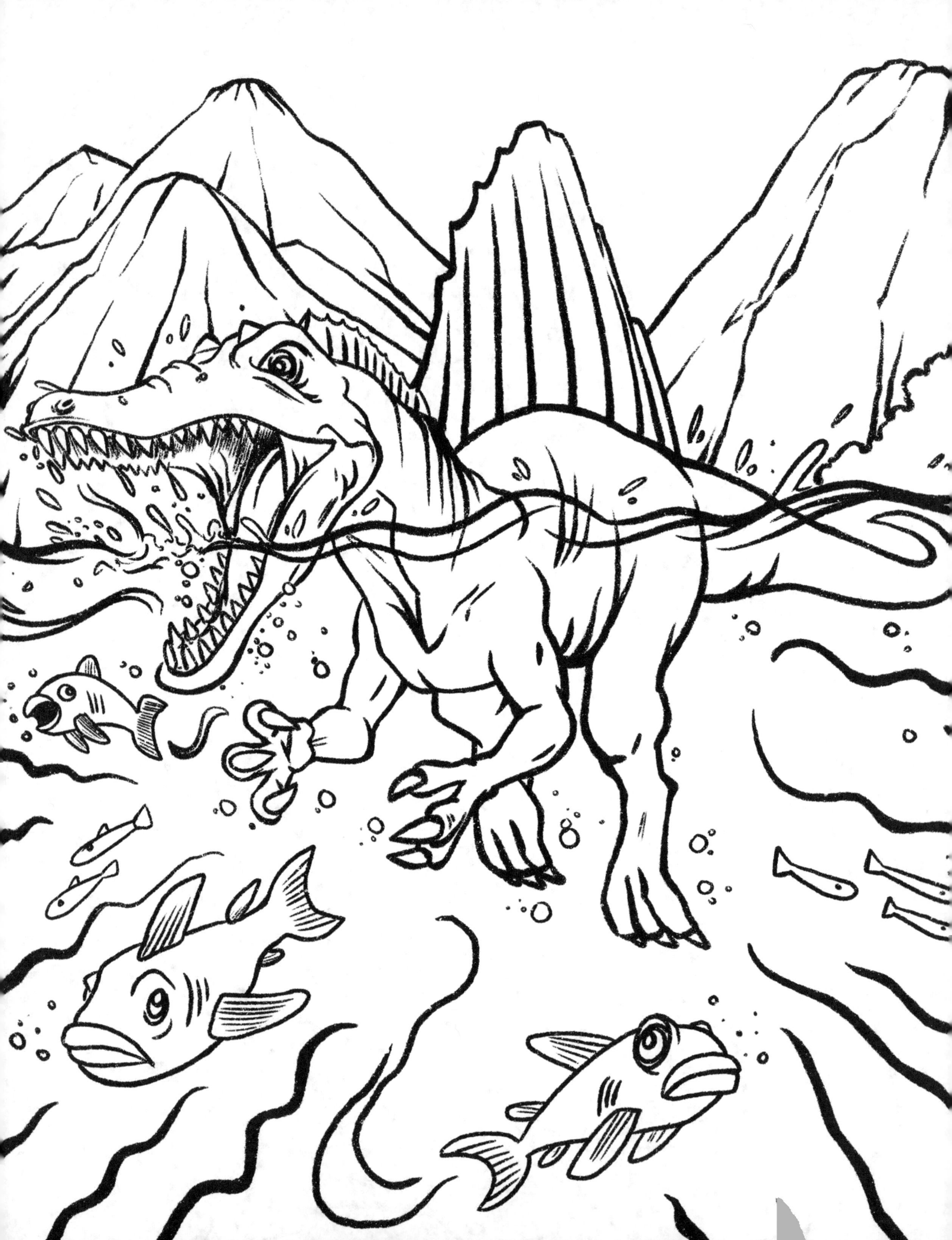

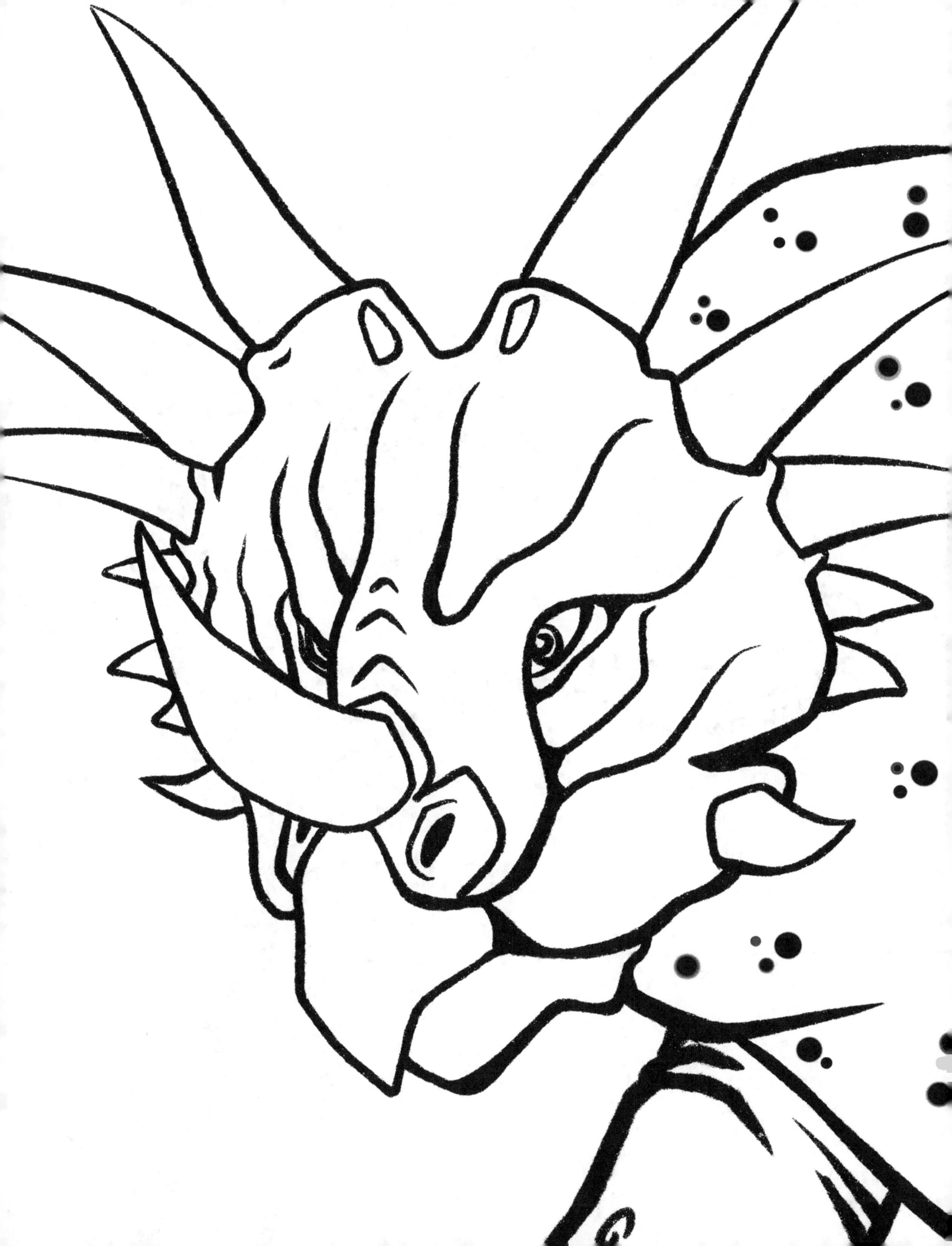

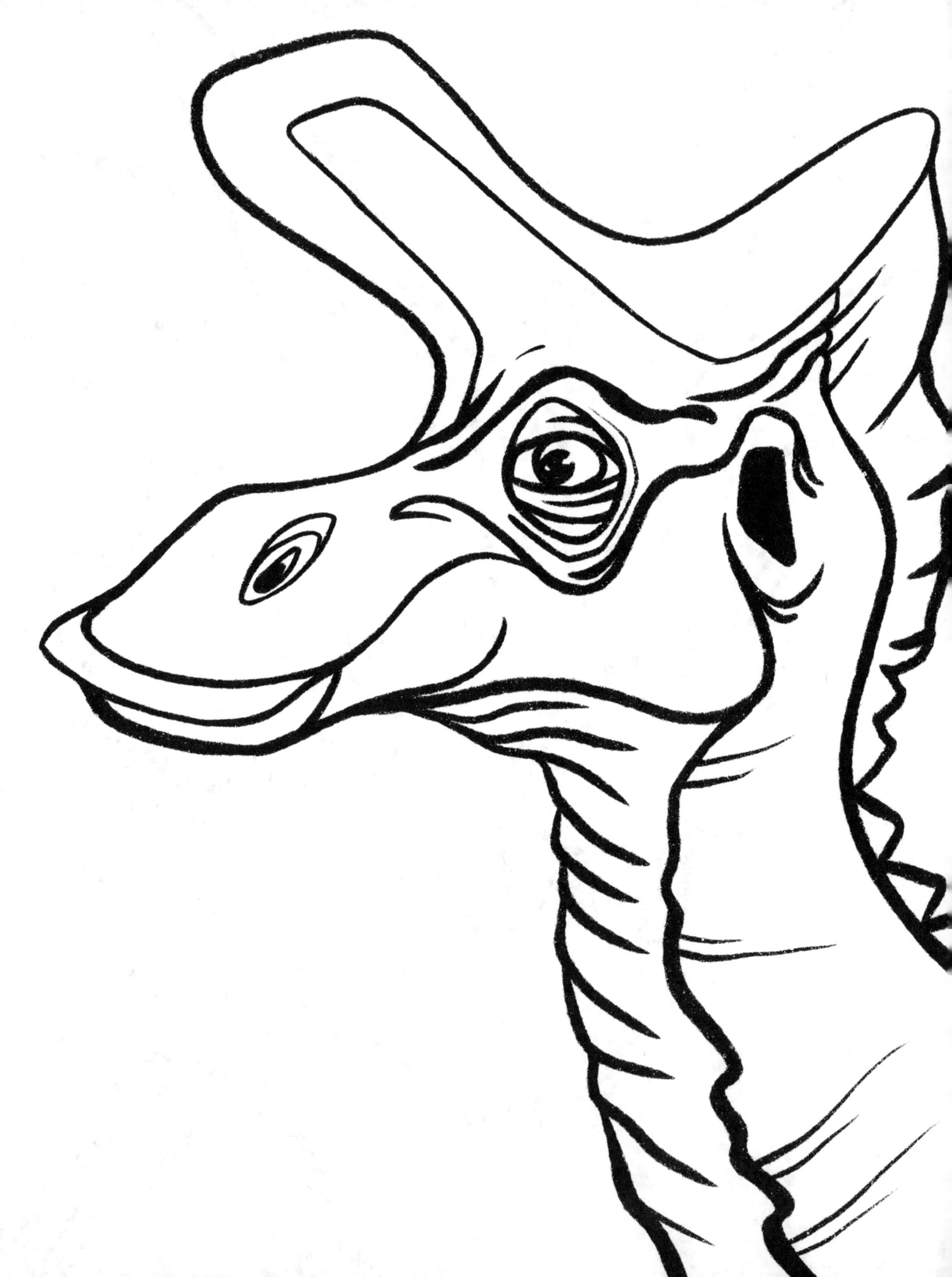

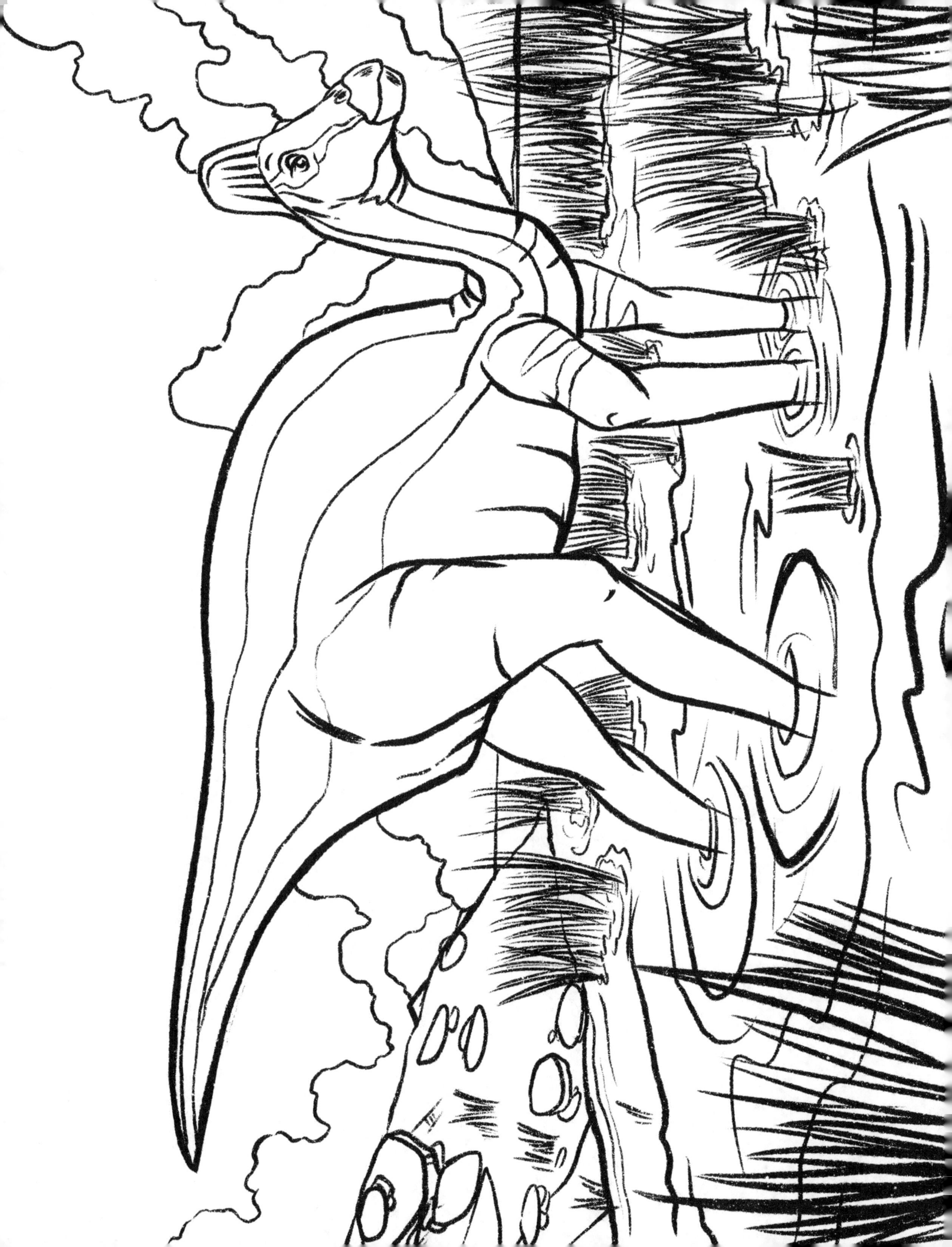